The Revenge of the Non-vegetarian

Upamanyu Chatterjee

SPEAKING TIGER

SPEAKING TIGER BOOKS LLP
125-A, Ground Floor, Shahpur Jat
New Delhi – 110049

First published in India by Speaking Tiger Books in 2018
This paperback edition published in 2022

ISBN: 978-93-5447-081-3

10 9 8 7 6 5 4 3 2 1

Typeset in Arno Pro by SÜRYA, New Delhi
Printed at Chaman Enterprises, New Delhi

Upamanyu Chatterjee is the author of the novels *English, August: An Indian Story* (1988), *The Last Burden* (1993), *The Mammaries of the Welfare State* (2000), which won the Sahitya Akademi Award for writing in English, *Weight Loss* (2006), *Way to Go* (2011), which was shortlisted for the Hindu Best Fiction Award, and *Fairy Tales at Fifty* (2014); the novella *The Revenge of the Non-vegetarian* (2018), which was shortlisted for the Crossword Jury Award; and *The Assassination of Indira Gandhi,* a collection of his stories written between 1985 and 2018.

In 2008, Upamanyu Chatterjee was awarded the Order of Officier des Arts et des Lettres by the French Government for his contribution to literature.

BY THE SAME AUTHOR

English, August: An Indian Story

The Last Burden

The Mammaries of the Welfare State

Weight Loss

Way to Go

Fairy Tales at Fifty

The Assassination of Indira Gandhi: Stories, 1985-2018

Villainy

For

Ranjit Mankeshwar

THE REVENGE OF THE NON-VEGETARIAN

In his first statement to the police, Basant Kumar Bal said that he had been woken up sometime in the middle of the night by the mooing of the cows. Not having a watch, he could not of course tell exactly when, but since in that household he could never go to bed before one in the morning, they, the Assistant Superintendent and the constable, would surely be able to deduce the hour of his awakening.

'And then?'

Even in his groggy state, Basant Kumar sensed several distinct things all together and at once: the fear in the mooing of the cattle, the heat and the glow, fierce and orange, at the open door of the shed, and above the mooing, somewhere, the frenzied, terror-crazed wailing of the dog. He arose from the mattress and fumbling, stumbling, groped for his slippers and put on his half-shirt and rushed out of the shed.

He gawked. It was not night but as though he had stepped inside the sun. The house of the Dalvis was on fire. The flames had swallowed up the entire single-storey building and rose, with a frightful rustle and roar, fifteen feet in the air. The heat physically pushed him back and for a few seconds, he could only gape; then, helplessly, in shock, he stumbled a few steps towards the well, paused, turned to move unsteadily in the direction of the cowshed, halted as with a distant boom something seemed to explode within the burning house and the hideous yelping of the dog rose in pitch to an agonized shriek before stopping, suddenly, in mid-scream.

'Go on.'

What should he do, what could he do? His

brain refused to work; he rushed to the well, slipped in the mud surrounding it, twisted his ankle. He drew water, then remembered that the two iron buckets were in the kitchen behind the wall of fire. He hobbled to the cowshed to unbolt its door, then out, as fast as his ankle would allow him, to the lane and the houses of the neighbours, before which, in a daze, in a croak of a voice that wouldn't carry, he, turning his head to left and right and up to the full moon, began to mouth whatever words came into his head. 'Fire. Help. Oh God. Fire. Save us. Have mercy. Help. Fire.'

MADHUSUDAN SEN, ICS, SUB DIVISIONAL Magistrate of Batia, could only visit the site of the ghastly occurrence late in the afternoon of the next day. He had been away on an inspection and received the information on the police telegraph a little after ten in the morning. Nadeem Dalvi, to whom the house belonged, had, till the previous month, been Sen's subordinate mamlatdar. Horrific news. A family of six, accidentally burnt to death, to cinders, at home just before the day they were to celebrate the engagement of the daughter.

The jeep chugged and honked its way

through the lanes of the small town. Stray children, trailing it, parroted its progress and echoed its din. Manjhi the driver knew the way. The police shooed the knot of idlers away to allow the jeep access. The loafers regathered around the vehicle like temporarily disturbed water.

'My God, there's nothing left.'

'Yes, sir,' nodded the Assistant Superintendent, 'a bad business.'

Sen and the policeman, surrounded by a handful of constables, stood at the gate of the Dalvi compound to survey what remained after the catastrophe. They saw walls blackened by soot, windows with neither glass nor frame, doorways with no doors. The four wooden posts of the verandah had been reduced to jagged, charred stumps, the tiles of the roof, shattered, singed, lay all anyhow everywhere, on the ground about the dwelling and inside, on the floor. The house, now open to the sky and its elements, itself looked aghast. The mango tree to the left of the verandah, black, burnt, stood tall and shocked like a dead sentinel. The sand and water used, ineffectually, to subdue the conflagration had turned its detritus to black mud.

With the constables leading, stumbling against one another and getting in the way, Sen and the Assistant Superintendent took a quick tour of the interior of the ruin. A large central room into which opened two other rooms and the spacious kitchen, to which was attached a windowless storeroom. The afternoon light, pouring in through the yawning roof and the door, and window-holes, fell delicately on the devastation. All that had been of wood—beds, tables, chairs—was now soot and cinders, stumps rising out of mud. The beds in fact had disappeared to reveal the iron trunks, now buckled and blackened, that had been stowed underneath them. Two wooden chests had exploded when the linen stored in them had caught fire. It had consumed everything, the dragon's breath, and found fodder in every nook—the curtains that partitioned off one half of a bedroom, the boy's schoolbooks, the mother's saris, the vats of mustard oil and ghee in the kitchen, the rice in the storeroom, the straw cushion that had been the dog's bed and most of all, the wood and coal kept at hand to stoke the kitchen fire.

They paused at the rear doorway, irresolutely, not sure whether the tour had ended. The kitchen seemed as though it had been bombed. From the doorway, Sen looked out on a nondescript courtyard that ended in a decrepit outhouse that shared one wall with the cowshed. Neither had been touched by the fire. He turned to amble about the kitchen, the constables again tripping over one another to get out of his way. He gazed long at the cracked bottles and the deformed tins, and peered with great interest into the black interiors of several aluminium pots as though to gauge the menu of the meal of the night before. The others waited patiently. At last, he turned to the Assistant Superintendent.

'And so?'

The policeman noisily cleared his throat before replying. 'The family comprised Dalvi and his Mrs, their daughter and a younger son, and Dalvi's widowed sister-in-law and *her* daughter. The sister-in-law and her daughter cooked and were housekeepers in general.' He coughed; his voice dropped a notch to signal a graver subject. 'The bodies were sent to Narasinh Nagar late this morning for a post-mortem, sir. Doubt, though, whether we'll get anything. They were just charred skeletons'—he raised his right hand to rub some invisible dust between forefinger and thumb—'powdery. Bits of black bone.'

'And the dog. And the servant? The one eyewitness to this ghastly event?'

The Assistant Superintendent glanced at the

doorway. 'Basant Kumar slept in the outhouse next to the cowshed, sir.' He hissed an order to a constable. The constable snapped to attention and ran out. 'We have his statement, sir.'

To the police, Basant Kumar maintained that the evening of September 29, 1949 had passed quite typically in the Dalvi household. The parents and the daughter had been discussing her engagement, the son had been trying to do his homework while listening to the radio, the sister-in-law and her daughter had been busy in the kitchen while he, Basant Kumar, had been occupied with his routine chores, ferrying in water and wood and coal, washing up, rushing to the bazaar to buy sugar and eggs, tending to the cows, clearing the clothesline, going off to get the boy's school uniform ironed, the usual. Never a moment's rest for him.

'Well, go on.'

Well, the family had had dinner at 9.30-10, as they did every day. Gosht of goat, daal, tamatar-paneer. *They* always ate well. Then the sister-in-law and her daughter ate in the kitchen, whatever was left over. He waited. They called him. He went and washed up the thalis, pots and pans and then, after they had all gone to bed, he had his dinner in the shed, whatever was left over for him by the sister-in-law and her daughter from whatever had been left over for them.

'So you never had enough to eat in that household, is that what you're saying?'

Basant Kumar protested. He said that he was not one to complain, for God had been most kind to him. But if one wants service from one's donkey, if one needs a beast to slave day in and day out, one must at least feed him adequately. The subject animated him. The Dalvis liked to eat, he stated. And they liked the others under their roof to feel want. His voice rose. 'They had non-vegetarian almost every day, saab, goat or chicken or fish or egg. They ate like rakshasas themselves and always left only two small pieces of meat in the pot, one each for the sister-in-law and her daughter.' His inhalations became audible, spasmodic. 'I got the scrapings of the pot, some gobs of curry, some grains of rice and a couple of chapatis. Then I'd have to filch two green chillis and one raw onion to complete my meal.'

'Where is the servant now?' asked Sen of the Assistant Superintendent. 'And the cows? You have of course spoken to all the neighbours? And the next of kin? I remember Dalvi telling me once of a younger brother who is an engineer at the Water Works on Indore Road.'

The policeman nodded. They stood in the rear courtyard just outside the kitchen. 'The brother was here this morning, completely shattered, sir, naturally. His man took the cows away.' He half-lifted his hand towards the outhouse before which stood, at attention, the constable who had left the kitchen on the orders of the Assistant Superintendent. 'Basant Kumar is here in bed, sir. He is not going anywhere.' The policeman made little effort to hide his grim amusement. 'He injured his ankle last night. Rather badly. A good sprain if not a fracture. And we'll be guarding this place for a while.' His voice dropped as he repeated, half to himself, 'No, he is not going anywhere.'

Basant Kumar was small, dark and moustached, with bulbous eyes that to Sen suggested an unstable temperament. In the gloom of the shed, lit inadequately by a kerosene lantern that cast fearsome shadows on the woodpile and the sacks of coal, he lay on his mattress and stared defensively at the law. 'He says that the pain in the ankle makes it impossible for him to stand, sir,' reported the constable in a soft bark that also suggested that he only awaited orders to raise the supine form upright with a couple of curses and a good kick.

The sharp smell of the kerosene remained distinct above the gentle stink of dung and animal urine that, permeating the planks of wood that separated the outhouse from the cowshed, diffused through Basant Kumar's living quarters like a blessing. A rexine bag atop the woodpile contained his clothes; on a nail hammered into the door—a plank, really—hung a rag of a towel and a half-shirt. Sen sniffed the stuffy air. Between the kerosene and the dung, he seemed to sense something else, raw onion, firstly, from the servant's exhalations, and yet another aroma, faint but heavy, suggesting meat fried and curried and cooked for an age in a hundred spices, as though for a rich marriage feast.

Basant Kumar looked exhausted, in pain, frightened and wary as he stared at all those uniforms crowding his space. Sen stood over him and smiled disarmingly. 'No, no, please don't get up,' he exclaimed even though the servant had made no move to do so. Turning to the Assistant Superintendent, Sen asked, 'Has he seen a doctor?'

Silently, with a wriggle of his eyebrows, the policeman asked the same question of the nearest constable. In response, the constable snapped to attention and began to glare without blinking at the wooden pole from which dangled the lantern. 'You'll get well soon,' Sen assured Basant Kumar with another smile and turning, led the way out. On the way to his jeep, the group paused once to gather around the blackened mango tree to allow Sen to finish tut-tutting over the extent of the devastation.

At the jeep, observing the group poised, as it were, on its toes, so eager was it for him to depart, he addressed it once again. 'I shall dispatch a report to the Collector immediately. And meet poor Dalvi's brother to see what else needs to be done'—and then specifically to the Assistant Superintendent—'Could someone take that poor fellow to the Trust dispensary? He might not be faking that ankle, you know.'

After disposing of the day's work, Sen reached home, as was his habit, closer to eight in the evening than seven. The Magistrate's residence, a rather charming late-nineteenth-century bungalow on Temple Road in the Civil Lines area, was a mere couple of kilometres away from his court, and Sen often preferred, despite the bother of a peon preceding—and a second following—him to shoo the citizenry of Batia away from the royal path, to walk the distance. In any case, at the junction of Durga Tank Crossing and Temple Road, he invariably descended from the jeep to stroll the remaining few hundred metres, never failing to warn Manjhi to crawl in first gear and retain his thumb on the horn because, as he explained to the grinning driver, he didn't want to be sitting in the jeep when it ran over one of the dozens of devotees who used the route as a short cut to the temple.

The Civil Lines area of Batia, dating from the time of the creation of the sub-division, was some seventy years old; the Dayasagar Adinath temple, at the summit of the knoll behind it, a little over a thousand. Circa 900 A.D., the man in charge of the local archaeological office had said, attributable to one of the last Yadava kings. 'Architecturally not very significant, though it does attract, sir, as you will see, thousands of pilgrims every year.'

Almost all of whom, from the railway station and the bus depot, found it most convenient to trudge up to the hospices on the hillock by way of Temple Road. In the past, though, the blessing of this facility had been available to them only sporadically. Before 1947, every now and then, some irate Sub-Divisional Magistrate (with the approval of his District Collector, of course), fed up with the trickle, throughout the day and throughout the year, of the faithful outside his bungalow—and moreover, one that swelled to a stream every April and October—would put up a board at the mouth of the road that read (in English), *No Thoroughfare,* and post a sentry in a tent alongside the notice, round the clock, whose duty it would be to encourage the devotees to trudge further down Durga Tank Crossing, past Subzi Mandi, and turn right at Chhindwara Gate to take Company Bagh Road to the hillock. A mere five kilometres more—not even—nothing, a trifle, if gauged as an expression of the depth of their faith.

The precincts of a temple are sacred, naturally. But that with time the range of its influence waxes in concentric circles to encompass the proximate world, Madhusudan Sen learnt only incidentally at the breakfast table on the second day of his arrival in Batia. That the patron deity of Dayasagar Adinath was more fiercely ascetic than most incarnations, reverential beyond compare of life in all its forms—this much Sen was vaguely aware of; but he had little idea of what living in His blessed shadow would involve.

Sen was served greasy aalu parathas and dahi on his first morning in the sub-division, and toast, cornflakes and milk on the second. 'This will never do,' he muttered to himself, there being no one else to complain to; he summoned Murari the cook.

'Eggs and sausages, liver, toast, fruit and tea was my typical breakfast in Calcutta,' he explained gently to the nervous man. 'Sausages, I can understand, might be difficult for us here. But the rest?'

'Sir (Murari's trembling lips made it sound like My Lord), the entire area from Dayasagar Adinath down to Durga Tank Crossing is vegetarian, sir. Meat, fish, eggs, liver, not allowed. Not even onions and garlic. Out of respect, sir.'

'Has a Government Resolution or Order been issued to that effect?'

Murari's disconcerted features showed that he was apprehensive about revealing that he had absolutely no idea.

'Never mind. I shall find out myself. And you? Are you vegetarian?'

Murari rolled his eyes towards heaven. 'God has been most kind, sir.'

'Not clear. In making you veg? Or non-veg?'

'We have been devotees of Dayasagar Adinath Prabhu for four generations, sir.'

'Good. That's very good,' said Madhusudan Sen, adding, 'And I'll tell you by this evening what to do from tomorrow about breakfast and dinner.'

—

At the gates of his bungalow, two peons, warned by the jeep of the Magistrate's imminent arrival, on foot, scurried up to bow. Ramlakhan, the senior by a decade, announced, while bent over, that Saab had a visitor. His existence having been proclaimed, a third shadow stepped forward from behind the banyan tree to incline his head a fraction less submissively than the peons.

'Arif Dalvi, sir, from the Water Works. Junior Engineer.'

Oh. Sen felt guilty that, after having dispatched a clerk to the Collectorate at Narasinh Nagar with his report, he had allowed himself to be distracted from the tragedy of his mamlatdar by other routine office emergencies. 'Please come.' They all moved together up the driveway, one peon leading, a herald holding aloft a lantern against the darkness, the Junior Engineer two deferential steps behind Sen, and the younger peon, bearing another lantern, bringing up the rear.

Sen gestured towards the bamboo cane chairs in the verandah. 'Please sit.' The other wouldn't, he knew it. 'Please have some tea.' He might, standing. Dalvi placed on the cane table a small jute bag that remained upright on the glass surface. Sen recognized in it the shape of one of his tiffin carriers.

'For your dinner, sir. If Sir so desires, I will pass on to the kitchen.'

The Magistrate was both annoyed—'Really, how could you think of food in the middle of such a tragedy!'—and touched—'But thoughtful of you to remember the needs of others at a time like this.' He turned to the two eavesdropping peons. 'You, please take this bag to the kitchen and you, please bring some tea for Engineer Saab.' He himself would have his Cutty Sark and one Gold Flake cigarette but in peace, after the other's departure.

'Beef stew, sir, made at home for Your Honour's degustation. And the meat is fresh, sir. My niece in fact—' Arif Dalvi's voice faltered here a little—'was to have married the son of the supplier.'

‘Thank you so much. Now please sit down and tell me how we may be of help in this tragic case. The police have already been instructed to be both speedy and thorough.’ In the light from the lanterns, Sen noted that Dalvi had his brother’s regular features but was shorter and plumper. He repeated his request three more times before the engineer obeyed and lowered himself to delicately balance his rump on the very edge of a cane chair.

‘I was to see my brother yesterday but couldn’t. I was delayed in Bhaichand Bazaar.’ The younger Dalvi addressed himself to the thousand insects orbiting the kerosene lanterns above the balustrade. ‘We had cooked at home a special beef stew—some of which I’ve brought this evening for Your Honour’s dinner’—a respectful glance here in the direction of Sen‘s knees—‘and my brother’s servant carried home for the household a vat-ful of it.’ He shrugged his shoulders. ‘I don’t even know if they could get to taste any of it.’

'Your brother was a most discreet, helpful and efficient colleague. I shall miss him terribly.' Sen sensed the return of the eavesdroppers; he waited for the tea to be served and then stared smilingly at the two peons till they melted into the darkness of the garden. Where they wouldn't stay for long, he knew, for fear of the snakes. 'He was the one I turned to first in an emergency.'

'His brothers and sisters, we all did, sir.'

IN THE FORENOON OF THAT SECOND DAY IN the sub-division, after his second vegetarian breakfast, Sen had chosen Nadeem Dalvi to speak to because he looked the capable sort and, just as important, was highly likely to be a meat-eater. 'Come in, shut the door, I don't want Adhikari eavesdropping behind that curtain, and sit down.'

Sen briefly explained the problem to his subordinate, so briefly that Dalvi continued to look blank. Sen took a deep breath and began again, the second time using as much Hindi as he could. 'I am by no means an irreligious man. In fact, you could say that my taste in food is strictly Vedic.' The wit, deservedly, was lost on his listener. 'I have been accustomed since childhood to some non-vegetarian item in every meal. Meat, fish, eggs, liver, beef.' Dalvi blinked once at beef but said nothing.

He took a quarter of an hour to grasp the matter, not because he was slow to follow but because he was thorough. He weighed each statement of his superior and assimilated it before moving on to the next. 'You know, Dalvi, if you don't eat well, you can't work well. Instead of focusing on your files and inspections, you would be daydreaming about food.' The mamlatdar also hinted at alternatives just to be certain that they had been properly considered before being dismissed. 'Well, frankly, I *like* the bungalow that's been allotted to me, those centurial trees, those arches, that picturesque well. I see no need to move to some newer, considerably less charming house in Civil Lines only to desist from offending—who *will*

I be offending, exactly, Dalvi, by eating a good mutton vindaloo at my own dining table?'

'Better not to find out, sir,' murmured Dalvi, staring not at the young face across the table but, since he had voiced disagreement with a superior, at the handsome clock on the green wall.

He learnt, during that first long conversation, that the new Magistrate was, despite his youth, a man of strong opinions, both cautious and intelligent, and quietly bullheaded. 'There exists no Government Resolution or Order declaring Temple Road a vegetarian zone, does there?' Sen paused to allow the mamlatdar to hem and haw and then continued, 'There doesn't. I have checked. What does exist is the vox populi. Which I as a responsible administrator do not wish to oppose or offend. And to think that seventy per cent of the country is, like you and me, non-vegetarian.'

At the end of their chat, they had decided,

more or less, on a course of action. Sen would pay Dalvi a sum of three rupees and four annas per week. Dalvi protested. Sen did not allow him to speak. The non-vegetarian stuff would be cooked at Dalvi's house ('We would be honoured, sir, my sister-in-law is, if I may be permitted to say so, not at all useless in the kitchen') and, suitably camouflaged ('Just put it in the office file bag'), ferried twice a day, on bicycle, to Temple Road by the mamlatdar's most trustworthy peon, also a Muslim. To lessen his subordinate's responsibilities, Sen told Dalvi not to bother with sea fish or chicken; for one, Bengalis ate only river fish and for another, chicken flesh was so tasteless that it made him *feel* vegetarian. Dalvi's man should buy eggs, rohu or kaatla or ilish fish, and red meat—goat, of course, and beef.

'The government is going to enact legislation—any time now, definitely this year—banning the slaughter of cows before they reach a certain age.' Sen waited for Dalvi to break into sobs. 'I certainly cannot break the law to indulge my food habits. So buffalo meat it shall be. And I must thank you for being so willing to help me out in what is after all an entirely personal matter.' He grinned at Dalvi's protestations and was embarrassed to remember, just when the mamlatdar had reached the door, yet one more concern. 'Oh Dalvi, I'm *so* sorry.'

The mamlatdar about-turned to present a face that was a mask of patient and polite enquiry. 'I need another cook,' confessed his superior. 'The temple—and not a lowly mortal's kitchen—is the place for one who considers touching onion and garlic a sin.'

A BATH WITH BUCKETS OF TINGLING WELL water, Cutty Sark and Gold Flake amongst the insects on the terrace, and dinner almost at ten. Arif Dalvi's stew was a meal in itself, reddish-gold in hue, richly aromatic, with potatoes, carrots and roasted and powdered cashew nut and a couple of unusual spices that Sen could not immediately identify. The transition from elder to younger Dalvi as principal protein and cholesterol supplier was, he saw, going to be smooth but, said he to himself, shaking his head over the beef, he could well have done without it.

Eavesdroppers have their uses; at morning tea on the second day after the incineration of the Dalvi household, Sen learnt from Ramlakhan that Basant Kumar the servant seemed to have given his guards the slip and, well, disappeared.

'Oh damn,' he muttered and, disgusted that the morning had been ruined, stretched forward to fiddle, in search of the seven o'clock news, with the knob of his prized Grundig transistor radio.

At tea again, on the sixth morning after the fire, he was informed, once more by the redoubtable Ramlakhan, that the post-mortem report had been dispatched from the Civil Hospital, Narasinh Nagar.

'Oh good,' murmured Sen and then, even while wondering why he was being sarcastic with the poor fellow, couldn't help adding, 'Hope they've marked you a copy.'

BASED ON A DETAILED VISUAL EXAMINATION OF the cadavers sent to him for analysis from Batia, the Civil Assistant Surgeon at Narasinh Nagar, Dr Shambhu Nath Baroi, drew the following conclusions:

> *Post-mortem has been conducted on all six corpses. The findings may be seen to fall into three categories: i) general condition of the bodies, ii) damage to soft tissue and internal organs and iii) damage to the skeletal structure.*
>
> *The burns in all six cases have been extremely severe, ranging from first- to*

fourth-degree, leading to excessive bleeding of the internal organs. The bodies in general are found to have curled up because of profound damage to, and the consequent diminution of, the muscles and tendons.

The internal organs on the whole are seen to be badly burnt and extremely reduced in size because of loss of fluid and their having been consumed by heat. In three cases, severe lacerations and rupture of the liver and the spleen, and complete severing of the aorta, are also to be seen.

In general, morphological findings in all six bodies range from local, superficial burns of the skin to calcined skeletal remains deprived of any enveloping soft tissue. Several large bones including the femur, tibia, fibula and humerus, the base of the skull, the cervical vertebrae, the hyoid bone and several ribs in the thoracic and lumbar region manifest fractures; the bodies, particularly the region of the skull, appear to have been repeatedly struck by a hard, heavy instrument, typically a spade or the back of an axe.

The cause of death in all six cases is severe trauma.

The fractures of the bones by a blunt instrument appear to be ante-mortem while the burns, it is indicated, are post-mortem in nature.

'WELL?'

Sen, surrounded by the policemen, now a gloomier lot, stood once again in the sunshine in the Dalvi compound. They had every reason to feel sadder and wiser; two of their constables, those guarding Basant Kumar on the night of his escape, had been, pending a detailed enquiry, suspended from service for dereliction of duty. And then the CID team from Narasinh Nagar, finding on arrival that the labour hired by Arif Dalvi had done a thorough job of cleaning up what remained of the house and compound, thereby wiping out any pointers to the sequence of events, had given the local police hell and continued to give them hell even after returning to Headquarters.

The Assistant Superintendent was barely coherent in his narration of events, so nervous and depressed was he. Sen paid him almost no attention while he recounted the official version of what had occurred; the Magistrate had already learnt from Ramlakhan the real story that morning. It was neither long nor surprising. The two guards that night, as every night, had been drinking. One had fallen asleep and begun to snore, the other had gone off to piss. When he'd returned, he, presuming that nothing had changed in his absence, had settled down, also to snore, at the doorway of the outhouse, without caring to check whether its occupant was still in there. They'd peeked inside the shed only upon waking well after sunrise.

'But tell me, this Basant Kumar's ankle really was fractured and his foot was in plaster? That is a fact and not a fabrication?' Sen glanced at the

Assistant Superintendent, who looked offended; not caring to hear his response, Sen continued, 'He couldn't have gone very far with that plaster.' He looked about him as though trying to put himself in the fugitive's place. He saw in turn the empty cowshed, the vacant outhouse, the stark skeleton of the mango tree, the well, the shell of a house, Arif Dalvi's idling labourers waiting to restart work on the remaining debris.

'The constables who are waiting for Basant Kumar at the railway station and the bus depot will fall asleep during their vigil and miss their promotions, so long will it take him to show up there.' He paused, in vain, to allow the policeman time to chuckle. 'I should think that he's here somewhere. Has someone, for instance, checked that well?'

Seventeen hours later, when one constable and one labourer lowered themselves into the well to heave up and out an unconscious, near-dead Basant Kumar, no one remembered to applaud Sen's prescience. He was too much of a gentleman to blow his own trumpet but he did murmur, once, 'I told you so' to the Assistant Superintendent's stone-deaf ears.

The policeman could not be blamed for giving his attention to more important matters. 'Handcuff him. I don't care. Three of you, take him, come with me to the Trust Dispensary.' He ordered a fourth constable, tall, pale, to strip and descend into the well to see what other treasures would come to light. He then slouched off to his jeep, pausing en route to nod at the knot of awed labourers. That was the closest that he could get to thanking them for drawing the attention, that morning, of the constable on duty to a funny, faint series of groans emanating, every minute or so, from the well.

The jeep trundled off, and two constables, some labourers, a few idlers encircled the well, peered into its dank gloom, silently observed the pale figure in singlet and striped underwear, cursing and muttering under his breath, descend the slippery rungs. They watched him become a lustreless blob, then disappear; then they heard him shout something that sounded reassuring, perhaps he wanted to inform the outside world that he had landed without mishap on the ledge just above the water. Familiar sounds next, of splashing and the clink and clang of the bucket, floated up to them. Then a shout, joyous, more commanding, and two sharp tugs on the rope. Galvanized, one of the labourers began pulling up, hand over hand, the bucket. The others, again silent, watched it surface out of the gloom. Wedged into it, with the rope lashed around it to keep it in place, was a large aluminium cooking vat, unwashed and foul-smelling, its insides brown and caked with meat curry that had gone off several days ago.

The constable, tall, pale, bobbed up soon

after, grinning with relief—and joy at not reappearing empty-handed—a second bulge in his singlet just above his paunch. Continuing to bare his teeth all around, he stepped gingerly out of the circle of mud surrounding the well, reached in and drew out from next to his skin a cloth pouch with a drawstring. Hefting it in his hand, he announced to the assembled, 'Two gold necklaces, bangles, earrings. The sisterfucker had the family jewels.'

Basant Kumar is on foot, pushing his bicycle; firmly lashed to its carrier is a large, covered vat of beef stew that he is ferrying home from Arif Dalvi's quarters. For two kilometres, its aroma has made him salivate, driven him mad as he weaves through the groups of townsfolk on their way to the Ramlila at Sahukar Maidan. At Bhaichand Bazaar, he buys provisions and asks the bakery to add an extra dozen kulchas to the Dalvi monthly account. After the level crossing, he gets off the road into Ghantai's sugarcane field. When he can't be seen by any passerby, he parks the bicycle on its stand, takes the vat off and places it carefully on the ground, sits down cross-legged himself and, with the kulchas, eats about a third of the meat. For twenty minutes, the only sounds around him are the hoot of a distant train approaching the level crossing, the clamour of birds returning to roost in their favourite trees, the tinkling of the bells of passing bicycles, the rustle of a bandicoot amongst the stalks of sugarcane and his own methodical, noisy chewing. The meat is soft, well-stewed. He masticates even the bones to powder, swallows them. He burps. It will soon begin to get dark. He burps again. He is sated, for five minutes, he cannot move or think.

With his fingers, he flattens the rest of the stew down to appear as though it has not been touched. It looks noticeably diminished, with curry stains all along the sides of the vat, going up to two inches below the lid, a clear marker of how much stew has disappeared. He grins, licks his fingers clean. He repacks the vat on the carrier of the bicycle and begins once again the trudge home.

He leaves the stew in the kitchen; at smelling the meat, the dog barks and dementedly wags its tail. Basant Kumar goes to the shed to fetch coal and wood for the evening's cooking. When he returns, Dalvi's sister-in-law, a fleshless, despondent thing, has removed the lid of the vat and is examining the stew.

'You seem to have eaten a lot of it on the way,' she remarks listlessly.

'Yes. I want some more. Not now but later.' And that is the truth but he surprises himself by revealing it. He is feeling strong. He senses that it is the meat.

She doesn't care to reply, begins putting away the provisions that he has brought back from Bhaichand Bazaar. The dog, unable to control itself, puts its paws up on the mud ledge and strains its snout to within an inch of the vat. Basant Kumar is shocked at that insult to his sense of himself; without even thinking, he smashes the log of wood in his hand down on the beast's skull. With a sort of half-yelp, it slides off the ledge, lands on the sack of coal, rolls off it. Basant Kumar brings the club down twice more on its head before turning to the speechless woman. Good, sturdy weapon, this, he thinks to himself as he begins on her.

He gets them all, one by one, in the course of a long evening. The sister-in-law's daughter next because she is startled by the agony in the dog's last yelp. The others are away; he waits for them, dragging, in the meanwhile, his three corpses about so that none is immediately visible from the front door.

Dalvi's son is the first home, back early from the Ramlila; his declamation of the more memorable lines from the performance is audible to Basant Kumar even while the boy turns in at the gate; he waits in the central room with the log of wood in his hand.

'Some shikanji, Basant bhaiya, quickly! I'm dying of thirst.'

'Something's happened to Tiger, in the kitchen, come and see.'

The club breaks on the boy's head, leaving him stunned, gurgling and choking and writhing beside the dog's corpse. Basant Kumar walks hurriedly to the outhouse to fetch the wood-cutting axe. On his return, he pauses in the kitchen doorway to breathe deeply and look about him. It is good, says he to himself, the timing of it, all the neighbours and other busybodies enjoying themselves at the Ramlila. So should I have been had I even one free evening to myself. He enters and shuts the boy up with one smart tap of the axe. He then moves from room to room to light the kerosene lanterns.

Mother and daughter he has half an hour for. They will take the six o'clock bus from Narasinh Nagar and then a tonga from the terminus; daughter will haggle with the tongawala outside the gate while mother with her problematic bladder will scurry off straight to the toilet at the back. Latch the door from the outside and take care of the daughter first.

'Something's happened to Tiger, in the kitchen, come and see.'

It doesn't quite work. She has never liked the servant, his sullenness and his staring eyes, she hardly talks to him, and he appears so peculiar this evening with that smile in his eyes, and is that the kitchen axe that he's hiding behind his right leg? 'Ammi!' she shouts for her mother, once, and then, most unexpectedly, about-turns to return to the safety of the outdoors. She is quick, already on the threshold when with a moan of desperation Basant Kumar darts forward a couple of steps and flings the axe at her. Its blade gashes her neck and shoulder, falls to the floor with a clatter. With a soft half-scream, half-groan, she stumbles, slumps against the door, takes long to fold up in a heap on the doormat that says WELCOME. He grabs hold of an arm and, leaving streaks of blood on brown doormat and red cement, drags her indoors. He hears behind him somewhere a door rattling and a female voice shouting, 'Yasmin! Yasmin!'

She is losing blood in spurts, is terribly conscious, in intolerable pain; he looks her in the eyes as he brings the axe down, repeatedly, on her chest and skull.

The mother's body he leaves to bleed in the toilet.

Dalvi himself he has to wait for till nine, when the retired mamlatdar returns from cards and carrom at the local club. Till then, from the lane and the neighbours' houses beyond the compound walls, Basant Kumar must be seen going about his chores—the well, the cows—and the household must appear normal—the radio is on, and a couple of times in the doorway, the servant turns to respond to a question from indoors. He is busy, he *does* have work to do. He adds rice to the stew and carries the vat away to the outhouse to be enjoyed later. He takes Mrs Dalvi's keys from her handbag, pulls out from under the bed and unlocks the small trunk and removes her pouch of jewels. There is other stuff concealed elsewhere, he knows, what with the daughter's engagement and the attendant excitement, but all that seems less important than arranging for a meat-stew dinner, in peace, in the wee hours.

He lights the two lanterns hanging in the verandah and scans the street beyond the low wall. Quiet, a few stragglers, everyone still at the Ramlila. To anybody dropping in unexpectedly, he will say that the family's gone off to Narasingh Nagar for some last-minute shopping for the engagement; no, visitors are not going to be a problem. With his back to the courtyard, he tries to see what Dalvi will see on his return. There is the daughter's blood on the threshold, the doormat and the verandah floor. Clean it up? But he doesn't much feel like a servant anymore. Something's happened to Tiger/your son/your daughter/your wife/your servant sister-in-law/ your servant niece. Come and see.

He puts out the lamp in the central room and returns outdoors, to face the street. Songs on the radio behind him, the programme of Hindi film hits that mother and daughter were both so addicted to. With the axe beside him like a faithful pet, he sits with his back against one of the pillars of the verandah to wait. It is restful. Dalvi arrives four songs later. Basant Kumar watches him come up from the gate. He is in a good mood, Dalvi, for even before he spots the servant in the shadows, he begins to hum along with the song from *Mahal* that is playing.

'Blood! This is blood? Whose blood?'

'Oh mine, saab. I nicked myself while chopping wood.'

'Well, clean it up! What'll people think? Where is everybody?' Dalvi strides off towards the kitchen, the servant at his heels, and is all at once dead still at seeing, before the sack of coal, the dog's corpse with its skull caved in. Then with that terrible blow to the back of his head, he lands with a great, clumsy thump on his beloved pet.

Liking working to music, Basant Kumar then rearranges the bodies once more, two in the kitchen, two each in the bedrooms, the dog in the central room. Shouldn't it look as though they tried to escape but just couldn't open any door or window in time? But they are *always* kept open, the doors and windows. Suddenly, he couldn't care less, he is terribly bored of the bodies. And tired. He sprinkles on them and on the furniture, the curtains and the woodwork kerosene, ghee, mustard oil, anything combustible that he can find. He places in every nook and cranny the coal, wood and cakes of cow dung stacked in the kitchen. Would that be enough? He gets more from the outhouse. At last he has finished; more accurately, he is exhausted, fed up.

Before locking up, he sits in Dalvi's armchair in the central room and, careful not to drop either match or ash anywhere but in the ashtray (the thought makes him giggle; imagine going up in smoke with them!), enjoys one of the mamlatdar's cigarettes. He then shuts the windows and bolts the doors but leaves the lanterns burning.

Outside, he sits down with his back against the mud wall of the cowshed, smokes a second Dalvi cigarette and waits for the night to lengthen. The house looks cheerful, with the windowpanes aglow in the light from the kerosene lamps. He will bide his time, for the pedestrian traffic in the lane will ease only after ten, and the lights in the neighbouring houses and the shops further down the road be extinguished closer to eleven. Then, in unhurried fashion, he will feast once more. He doesn't see himself kindling the Dalvi household before two in the morning. A leisurely night.

JUST BEFORE THE GRAND ARCH AT THE FOOT of the hillock, the Dayasagar Adinath Temple Trust ran—still runs—for the well-being of the pilgrims and the public weal, a dispensary; so useful was it that within three years of its institution in 1904, it grew to become a modest but busy twelve-bedded hospital. It was to that dispensary that the police jeep rushed the unconscious Basant Kumar.

The Assistant Superintendent himself having escorted the patient, there was no question of the doctor on duty, by name Kesari, asserting that they were full up—they always were—and that the jeep had better continue on its way and cart its responsibility to the Civil Hospital at Narasinh Nagar. Within minutes, a thirteenth bed was organized at the end of the corridor on the first floor and to it was shifted an old woman with all the symptoms of both heatstroke and jaundice and no clout. Basant Kumar was trundled to her place and, after having had his pulse and pressure taken, began receiving glucose intravenously.

His eyelids fluttered open at dawn next morning, he saw around his bed two human forms, blurred, in khaki, asleep and snoring (yet again); he shut his eyes. The Assistant Superintendent was at the dispensary at eight, demanding of the doctor on duty, by name Bijoria, that the patient being out of danger, he release him in order to allow the police to ferry him to the Civil Hospital, Narasinh Nagar, for a thorough medical investigation.

Instead, they took Basant Kumar to the Batia police station, stripped him naked and made him stand in the midst of four constables. With his baton, the Assistant Superintendent tapped him hard on his shin above the plaster and said, 'We will now take off the plaster and I will play knock-knock with my stick on your hairline fracture. Would you like that? If not, then I suggest that we seek time from the Magistrate and you explain to him that for some meat and some jewels, you bludgeoned to death your employer, a retired Revenue official, a pillar of the community, and five innocent members of his family. Then, to destroy the corpses and all evidence, you burnt them. You set fire to them and to their household, destroying life and property in the most inhumanly cruel manner. Is that an adequate summary of the events of the night of September 29, 1949?'

Basant Kumar scratched an insect bite on his sallow, distended stomach. He said nothing.

'You will sign a statement in the presence of Magistrate Saab.' The Assistant Superintendent pushed his baton under the chin of the accused and gently prised his head up so that he could stare into his eyes. 'He will ask you if you are being coerced into confessing. If you embarrass me in his presence, we will have to return here so that I can examine your hairline fracture. Is that clear?' After five seconds, he added, 'I want to see a nod and hear a Yes.' He paused till he got the first. 'You sign that confession in court and I'll get you some top-class non-veg from Shantaram's Lunch Home.'

Basant Kumar put on his clothes and they let him sleep a couple of hours in the lockup; they then asked him to shave and freshen up with water from the hand pump. From Som's dhaba next door, they brought him bread- and gobi-pakodas and tea. He wolfed everything down.

In the afternoon, the Sub-Divisional Magistrate first heard the three cases scheduled for that day before turning to the matter that had brought the Assistant Superintendent to his court. Madhusudan Sen first asked the peons to shoo away the idlers crowding the two open doors of the courtroom; he then regarded, expressionlessly, the small, moustached man standing in the corner handcuffed to a swarthy constable. He watched Basant Kumar's bulbous eyes flit from one inanimate object in that hall to another—from a peon's turban to the railing before the Magistrate's desk, thence to the steps leading up to the dais on which he sat—unable to look at anything that could look back. Sen showed no sign that they had met before. The accused's eyes glanced up at him for a second when he began speaking and, as though scalded, ricocheted away again.

'I hope you know why you're here.' Sen tried to avoid looking sheepish on account of his atrocious Hindi. 'I understand that you want to make a confession in my presence. It will be recorded and, based on what you say, a statement prepared. You'll have to sign it. I too will record that it was made in my presence.' He paused. It didn't appear from Basant Kumar's features as though he had paid attention to a single word. 'Have you followed what I said?'

'Answer, you!' suddenly growled the Assistant Superintendent, startling everybody in the courtroom. 'The Honourable Magistrate has asked you a question!'

Looking down at the handcuff on his right wrist, Basant Kumar, after an interminable fifteen seconds, and barely perceptibly, nodded.

‘If you are being intimidated in any way by the forces of the law,’ continued the Magistrate, not feeling honourable in the least at that moment, ‘you have a right to refuse to confess. You should be forewarned that any statement that you sign in my presence may be used in evidence against you.’ His will began to peter out in face of the dejection and disinterest in the accused’s very posture; but not for nothing, he reminded himself, was he part of the steel frame of the country. He soldiered on. ‘Furthermore, I would have to certify that you, the subject, have confessed of your own volition, without any coercion. I cannot do that unless it is the truth.’ He paused again; even the punkah above his head, it seemed, creaking back and forth, seemed unable to mask its embarrassment at the ridiculousness of his utterances. ‘The court clerk will inform you now of the procedure relating to criminal proceedings, the FIR, the Investigating Officer’s Report, then you will appear before a Judicial Magistrate who will take cognizance of the crime, a charge sheet would be prepared, you'd have to spend some time in judicial custody in prison awaiting trial, and the hearing itself in the court of sessions—all that you may expect in the days—I should say years—to come.'

That the Assistant Superintendent was so carefully not looking at him told Sen, more clearly than anything else, how much he was wasting his breath speaking of justice to a murderer of six innocent humans.

NARASINH NAGAR'S PRINCIPAL JAIL, LOCATED on, well, Jail Road, dates from 1916. Over the years, it has risen in status from medium- to maximum-security prison to Central Jail, the improvement in rank mainly denoting higher boundary walls topped by an extra two rows of barbed wire and a marginal increase in the annual budget from a second source under Recurring Heads of Expenditure. Having attained the prestige of a Central Jail, it must now also, as per norms, boast of a rehabilitation programme for its inmates. But in October 1949, it was simply the main penitentiary and house of incarceration of the second most populous city in the region, with eight wards, three barracks per ward and an average of thirty prisoners per barrack. Basant Kumar Bal entered it on October 21, 1949 and stayed there, in the first phase, for four years, six months and eleven days, awaiting trial.

He was allotted Barrack B of Ward 6. His immediate neighbours were, in the language of the police files, habitual bad characters—several housebreakers, two bootleggers, one forger, two embezzlers, three kidnappers. They disregarded him. They didn't much like murderers, particularly one who had killed six people because he had wanted for himself their share of dinner, and then burnt the bodies because—so the bruit had it—he liked the smell of cooking flesh. He didn't mind being ignored; more accurately, he kept to himself, he didn't even see that they too kept away.

The dullness of the daily routine moreover suited him. Up at six (or earlier in summer, with the sunrise) for roll call, some dishwater tea and watery gruel for breakfast, back to the barracks. Freed again at ten in the morning to wash themselves, their clothes, their plates. Then hang about to observe those prisoners who needed to visit a hospital, or be present in court, exit the jail, handcuffed, with a posse of policemen. Locked up again till twelve, then lunch—watery khichadi, ditto potato curry, more chilli powder than potato. Confined again from one to three in the afternoon. Three to five, recreation—shuffle about in the courtyard in front of Wards 3 and 4, sit around in groups on the ground, kick a pebble about. Roll call again at sunset, dinner at 6.30, locked up for the night. Every day. For four years, six months and eleven days. In the first phase.

But he was not uncivil. He responded when spoken to, particularly when the interlocutor was a jailor or a warden. How come he had no visitors? he was asked. He couldn't think of anyone who would visit him. He had no family to speak of, he had left his village, in Purulia, on the death of his mother, some twelve years ago. As and when your case comes up in court, he was advised, plead Not Guilty. Say you were framed, it's the brother who did it, that the cops terrorized you into signing that confession. The court will probably assign you a lawyer. He certainly won't come here to see you but he might meet you for the first time for a couple of minutes in court on the first day. Plead temporary insanity. Think about it. You hadn't had meat for so long that something snapped in your head. Then you might get life. Life in jail, you'll agree, is better than death. Basant Kumar nodded.

When he passed, or saw, the boundary walls of the prison a dozen times a day, he did not wonder what was going on in the world beyond them, whether anyone remembered him. He was not that kind of human being.

WITH EACH PASSING DAY, THAT WORLD outside the prison remembered the servant less and less. As Investigating Officer, the Assistant Superintendent of Police of Batia finished his interviews with and recorded the statements of neighbours and other witnesses of the fire, analysed the sequence of events, studied and referred to the post-mortem report, the accused's several interviews to the police and his confession before the Magistrate, sought clarifications on seven legal and sixteen procedural issues from the Public Prosecutor and at last wrapped up and submitted his report to the Superintendent of Police of Narasinh

Nagar in early February, 1950. By April of the same year, the Judicial Magistrate (First Class) of Batia examined the papers sent by the police, formally took cognizance of the crime and, acknowledging that an offence had taken place, forwarded the case to the District and Sessions Court at Narasinh Nagar to initiate proceedings for the filing of a charge sheet.

Summons were issued to witnesses—neighbours, relatives—and interested parties and, along with police officials and the accused, the court heard them all between November, 1950 and January, 1952. Basant Kumar first stepped out of jail to attend court on November 16, 1950. He felt strange, unprotected, outside the prison walls; even in the gloom of the police van, the air felt different, shivery.

The journalists frightened him. He alit from the police van, handcuffed to a constable, and they surrounded him like stray dogs about to attack a cur who has wandered into their territory; they took photographs, shouted questions, followed him, baying, as he was led away up the steps and down the corridors. A tall, thin, balding man in an advocate's dress accosted him amidst the din and the jostle to bark into his ear, 'We will plead Not Guilty. You will say you were sleeping. You don't know who did it.'

—

The charge sheet; the trial. Hearing commenced on May 2, 1954. The judge, with his large spectacles, high forehead, taciturn manner and perpetual frown, petrified Basant Kumar. Day after day, the accused stood in his corner, handcuffed, steadily sweating, stealing glances at the drama of the moment, vaguely thinking that everything would be okay, he would get through the day only if he succeeded in not looking anyone in the eye. When he returned to prison in the late afternoon exhausted and afraid, less of death somehow than of living, someone, a pickpocket or a cheat, would ask, 'So how did it go?'; he wouldn't respond, just shrug his shoulders, he couldn't say, he didn't know.

In leisurely fashion, over a year and a half, no doubt arguing to himself that every day delayed in the case was a gift to his client of yet one more day of life, the defence lawyer, Bachan Lal by name, in his cross-examination of the witnesses for the prosecution, repeatedly pointed out that, on that fateful evening, none of them had actually seen either the accused with the victims or the house being set fire to by him. He, Bachan Lal, was reprimanded twice by the judge, once for insinuating that the slurred speech of Dr Baroi of the Civil Hospital, the author of the post-mortem report, was the result not of a stroke suffered several years ago but of excessive tippling; and the second time for hinting that the police had not probed at all the links between the murders and the consequent inheritance of the property and effects of the deceased by his younger brother, Arif Dalvi.

All in all, he did not perform too badly, Bachan Lal, particularly when one considers that his client was unable to pay him a single anna for his services; that doubtless was one reason why, after that initial fourteen-second meeting in the corridors of the court, he did not feel the need to talk to Basant Kumar again.

'I HAVE THREE REASONS FOR THIS VISIT, SIR. One: to thank you in person for your most manful and honourable act in shutting down that disgraceful abattoir against which we have been complaining since 1939. Two: to bemoan the terrible news. I understand that you are under orders of transfer. On promotion of course but—'

'No need to thank me, Mr Daftari, for doing my job,' replied Madhusudan Sen, smiling modestly. 'Though that abattoir was quite a shock, I can tell you.'

He did not add that he had come upon it by accident, really. Repairs to the State highway had necessitated their taking the old Canal Road to Narasinh Nagar for a meeting at the Collectorate. And then just after the Gaindapur level crossing, he had been assailed, almost physically, by a stench so powerful—of carrion, of rotten flesh and hot glue—that his stomach, for the first time in his life, had actually heaved.

'My god, Manjhi, what *is* that stink!'

But to Mr Sarat Daftari, Vice Chairman of the Dayasagar Adinath Charitable Trust, his response continued to be appropriately official. 'They had no permissions or licences from any authority. I'm sure that the police and the revenue officials would continue to be vigilant even after I move out.'

'From the hillock where we are, from the terrace to the west of the meditation halls,' said Mr Daftari, with a smile that suggested that the subject was no laughing matter, 'you get a fine view of the kites hovering—and the vultures waiting—over that shed where they boil the bones down for the button factory.'

‘That’s been sealed too,’ grinned Sen, pleased with his efficiency and thus ceasing to be magisterial. ‘It wasn’t a pleasant experience, not even for my coarse, non-vegetarian sensibility.’

IT HAD IN FACT BEEN QUITE NIGHTMARISH. AT the mouth of the shed, two butcher apprentices, swarthy adolescents, pulled a buffalo calf off a tempo by its forelimb; it broke its leg in the fall and not being able to get up, lay trembling on the ground, thrashing its legs about, excreting out of fear and mooing as much in agony as that terror. One of the young men caught hold of its tail and began to drag it into the shed; the other pulled a second calf off the mini-truck, also breaking its foreleg. Sen and the constable on duty followed the first calf, watched its head bounce, repeatedly, off the pebbles on the uneven ground, its eyes, distended by its distress, seemingly about to pop out of their sockets.

The cement floor of the shed was slippery with excrement, blood, offal and gore. Inside, it hit them like a hard slap on the head, the din of the animal world giving voice to its terror—the mooing of cattle sensing slaughter, the bleating of goats about to have their limbs broken and their blood drained out of gashes in their throats, hens in cages, clucking in frenzy seconds before being pulled out and beheaded. Sen himself, gazing about him, felt totally unmanned at all that carnage, those bits of skin and hair and clumps of crimson flesh scattered all over the floor. And the stench was frightful; the terrible fetor from the vicinal boiling house for the button factory mingled with the permanent smell of fresh, raw meat, of animal excrement, blood and fear and the sweat of the butchers.

The constable edged past Sen to accost a couple of men approaching them down the aisle between the poultry coops. Their kurta pyjamas, though well worn, were not stained with crimson; perhaps proprietor and son, thought Sen, the young man who was to have married Nadeem Dalvi's daughter. The constable barked something, doubtless the identity of the unexpected visitor, in the older man's ear. The latter's demeanour changed instantly; he straightened up and beaming, scurried forward. The Sub-Divisional Magistrate had of course dropped by to pick for himself some choice cuts. From the corner of his eye, Sen observed the calf that had preceded him into the shed being prepared for its future. Four butcher apprentices held its legs, flipped it over and tied its limbs tight to two poles, like a gymnast's parallel bars, above its head. The young man who'd dragged the animal in then, to loosen its skin by shrivelling it, drenched it, from an enormous vat, from head to toe in boiling water. The other three, laughing and shouting in jocular alarm, jumped back out of range. The shrieking of the calf made Sen's spine tingle, his teeth twinge. This is for the likes of me, this unspeakable savagery and torture; this blood sport with sacred life is but to create some cutlet or curry or kebab for the dinner tables of the carnivores.

'Salaam, morning. No thank you, just dropped in to see how you all can breathe around here...Could you show me your operating licence from the Revenue Department, please?'

'THE THIRD REASON FOR MY TAKING UP YOUR time this morning, Mr Sen, is to request you to visit the temple before your departure and share a meal with us.' Mr Daftari waited for the Magistrate to jump out of his chair with joy at the offer. 'It will give us a chance to be of service in assisting you to experience how wholesome and flavourful vegetarian cuisine can be.'

Nothing in a small town remains a secret for long; no doubt the bush telegraph of the bungalow peons, on the very day of the closure of the abattoir, had spread the news that the Sub-Divisional Magistrate had turned vegetarian. Arif Dalvi had showed up at the house that same evening, ostensibly to ask whether he should procure some fish and meat from Narasinh Nagar for the Honourable non-vegetarian but in point of fact actually to gauge the lie of the land, and to see whether it would be at all possible to get the Magistrate to rescind his order.

He couldn't even broach the topic; he didn't have the courage. Having had his Cutty Sark before Dalvi's arrival, Sen Saab was uncharacteristically loquacious that evening. And it was while he was babbling to the engineer about the horrors that he had witnessed at the slaughter-house that morning that the contours of the problem floated up into his consciousness like a submarine emerging out of grey water. 'I kept thinking while I was watching them butcher that calf, that your brother and his entire family lost their lives because of that very meat. And the deaths don't end there because I at least am not going to rest—or eat non-vegetarian—until Basant Kumar is hanged. So how far...?'

And it was the same question that Madhusudan Sen posed to the suave, elderly man-of-the-world from distant Bombay. 'How far, Mr Daftari, would you carry your reverence for life?' He smiled deprecatingly at the gentle incomprehension on the other's face. 'Would all vegetarians, for instance, be opposed to the death penalty for even the most despicable murderer? That is what we could chat about at the lunch that you have so graciously invited me to. Because it is not quite clear to me, the link between the carnivore and the love of slaughter. One thinks, you know, of the horrors inflicted on Europe and the world in the last decade by a vegetarian,' he abruptly opened a file that lay before him on his table and began flipping through it, not because it was urgent, not because he wanted to signal that the interview was over but because he all at once felt silly; he didn't know his interlocutor well enough to say what he was saying to him, but he continued, without looking up from the papers, because he had always been one to finish what he had started, 'and one senses there quite the opposite of a reverence for life.'

At daybreak on June 24, 1951, Madhusudan Sen left Batia for the last time. It would have been too hot after eight in the morning to drive to Narasinh Nagar to catch the train to the state capital at Nandanpur, hence the departure with the sky starting to blush and Manjhi the driver unshaven and yawning unabashedly.

A sizeable crowd, even at that hour, had gathered to see him off. He had been popular, and moreover the first native member of the Indian Civil Service to serve at Batia. His office staff was present, of course, holding bouquets and garlands, uncertain of when to hand them over, shuffling their feet and avoiding his gaze;

representatives of other departments as well, and the Secretary of the Dayasagar Adinath Trust and the Treasurer of the Carrom Club. The Assistant Superintendent of Police had dropped in to say goodbye the previous evening but sent his Station House Officer over at five in the morning; and in a corner of the verandah, hiding his tears behind a pillar, stood Arif Dalvi.

Sen shook hands, and exchanged a word or two, with each and every one present. Some were moved to lunge to touch his feet; role model that he was, he stopped them well in time, and in a firm but kind manner. Only with Dalvi did he merely nod once before passing on. He really had nothing more to convey to him.

'You'll have to be my eyes and ears, as they say,' he had told Dalvi at nine the previous evening when, in the confusion of supervising the packing of the last of his effects, they had stood together in the verandah to watch the first truck chug out of the driveway. 'I can't think of anyone better placed to do so. You have to watch the case, follow it, for a decade or two, perhaps even more. It was never in our hands, I know; it won't, I trust, for that reason, slip out of our memories.'

At nine forty, he forced upon Dalvi two aalu parathas, some mango pickle and a third cup of tea. 'Goyal the Sessions Judge has a fine medieval mind. He will hang him. No matter how many years he takes to pass judgment. Being a sentence of death, it would go to the Nandanpur High Court to be confirmed.' Sen shut his eyes and massaged his temples with the tips of his fingers. It helped him to focus. 'You'll have a decision and a case number; you can then track the matter at the High Court Registry. You'll know over the years when it comes up for hearing, when the court appoints another lawyer for the defence, what it finally decides.' He suddenly stood up, again tense and distracted by his departure, and not at all certain of Dalvi's competence. 'Do you understand what I'm saying? I'm going away to a new place, another job, a different world. I would need you to ensure that for *two decades,* I do not forget how your brother died.'

In the case of Basant Kumar Bal versus The State of Narmada Pradesh, in a sixty-three-page document, Judge Shyamlal Goyal pronounced his verdict on February 7, 1956.

Early in the judgment, he invoked the deity whose devotee he was.

> *It is to be noted that these ghastly murders took place virtually at the foot of the most blessed abode of Dayasagar Adinath Prabhu. They are thus not only a hideous and appalling crime against humanity but they also, if I may use the expression in connection with the divine, cock a snook at*

One whose all-pervading reverence for life, in all its forms, is the one dharma, the one law, that his votaries are enjoined to follow. The perpetrator therefore is more than devilish, he is fundamentally Godless…

I specifically asked the accused whether he is, as his name would suggest, a practicing Hindu. He said nothing in response, merely after a moment shrugged his shoulders. It is in keeping with his inherent wickedness that he butchered and burnt six innocent human beings because he, inter-alia, wanted to enjoy, all by himself, an entire pot of a preparation of ***beef****, a meat the consumption of which is forbidden to all Hindus.*

And in his ferocious butchery, he has not cared to pause to think of how he has also attempted to slaughter the characters of his victims. For we have heard several witnesses in this court. By all accounts, without exception, the deceased Mr Nadeem Dalvi was a pillar of the community, loved and respected by all, a model civil servant when in service and a generous and kind employer who was unfailingly considerate and humane in all his relations and dealings—with servant, neighbour, colleague, fellow citizen. It has pained this court to hear that sterling nature being consistently maligned; the impression sought to be created is that he was mean-spirited enough to half-starve his employee and not provide him three square meals a day, because of which the accused, deprived of adequate nourishment, became mentally so disturbed, so aggrieved, that he was in a sense, goaded, compelled, to retaliate in this hellish fashion. Frankly, we are not convinced of this revenge-of-the-non-vegetarian theory; it smacks more of emotive stratagem than cogent reasoning.

It appears in fact an open-and-shut case of murder most foul for gain. The accused coveted the jewels accumulated by the family for the daughter's approaching marriage. He was no doubt caught red-handed while stealing them and so, to escape detection, he killed the witness to that crime; then he butchered the others to cover up the first homicide. And ***then****, heartless and satanic that he is, he sat down amidst the corpses to make a meal of* ***their*** *non-vegetarian dinner.*

We have heard all parties, we have weighed the evidence; we are led to conclude that in this most heinous of despicable crimes, the culpability of the accused has been established beyond doubt. Under the provision therefore of Section 354 (5) of the Code of Criminal Procedure of 1898, Mr Basant Kumar Bal is to be hanged by the neck till he is dead.

BASANT KUMAR BAL SPENT THE NEXT seventeen years of his life in the central jail of Narasinh Nagar. He did change rooms though, for Section 30 (2) of The Prison Act of 1894 states that a prisoner sentenced to death must be kept apart from other prisoners, that is, from those awaiting trial and those behind bars for just a length of time, two years or fifteen or thirty. It is true that in the case of Basant Kumar, the judgment of death of the sessions court would first need to be confirmed by the Nandanpur High Court—and that process could take anything from a year to a decade—but the prison administration felt—and told the condemned man as much—that in his matter, the chances of the sentence being commuted to life imprisonment were less than zero. So better to move to death row early; there, he could settle down properly to wait for the warrant of execution.

They marched him out from Barrack B of Ward 6 to Barrack A of Ward 1 on March 4, 1956. The inmates of Barrack B, some of whom had known him for seven years, watched him go without a word. Meshram, the eternally jovial warden, led the way. Barrack A of Ward 1 was segregated from the rest of the prison by a wall and barbed wire. They entered the gate but first turned left to cross the barren courtyard to stop at a second gate, locked; beyond it stood a grey, single-storey structure with a domed roof and no visible windows.

'Kneel, touch your forehead to the foot of the gate,' ordered Meshram, smiling, 'and pray. I always first bring here those prisoners awaiting hanging so that they can pray and calm themselves into the right frame of mind.' He waited for Basant Kumar to carry out his instructions. 'Bend more! Your forehead should rest in the dust!' He castigated the prisoner, but merrily. 'Otherwise it shows that you are not humble at all before the gallows. But you will be, you will be—' one could hear in his voice a waggish, admonishing forefinger—'when at five in the morning, you haven't slept a wink all night, you hear the frightful crash of the trapdoor inside as it falls open to allow one of your friends in your new lodgings more room to dangle in peace. You can't fail to hear it no matter where you are in Barrack A. Get up now...' Suddenly bored, peremptory, but he regained his good cheer by the time they reached the entrance of the prison block—'Best alarm clock in the world, that trapdoor crashing open. You hear it once, you wake up every morning at five, trembling, because you heard it in your dreams.'

There were three other men in the large room to which Basant Kumar was brought, two rapist murderers, he learnt later, and one child kidnapper-killer. All three of them, coincidentally, were vegetarians. Hello, gomaas-a-haari, is how they greeted him. Beefeater.

Of the next seventeen years of his life, Basant Kumar spent twelve in that room. The vegetarians on the whole were kind to him. They called him Gomaas Kumar, found it amusing. They knew stuff, and when in a good mood, shared with him their understanding of things.

'You wash my clothes this week, Gomaas, and I'll tell you how long you have to live.'

He did, and learnt:

'At least four years, give or take another five. No one is going to touch you—except us—while the Nandanpur High Court ponders, and those judges take so long to examine and take stock that it gives potatoes and other tubers enough time to grow between their Honourable toes.' Two of the vegetarians, one rapist-murderer and the child kidnapper-killer, knew a fair amount of law. 'They will confirm death, of course. Do you have a lawyer?' Basant Kumar shook his head. 'Good. They are even dirtier than your non-vegetarian excrement because they suck you dry of whatever money you have. When the High Court judgement gets to you, file a Special Leave Petition in the Supreme Court. That will give you a further four years, give or take yet another five. Looks like a long life ahead of you, Gomaas bhai. If we are around, we'll prepare that Supreme Court SLP for you. If we are around.'

Only one of them was, though—to wit, the younger rapist-murderer—on September 8, 1962 when the High Court at Nandanpur confirmed the conviction and sentence of death of the lower court. The other two had moved on, one in the winter of 1959 and the other five months later.

Basant Kumar, on both occasions, had slept through the crash of the trapdoor next door.

The surviving rapist-murderer moved into top gear on the very day that the Narasinh Nagar jail received the judgment. It tickled him to have Basant Kumar follow him about, as a stray dog would a neighbourhood servant who at times throws it some scraps. 'C'mon, get your papers. And pray that the jail superintendent is in a good mood. He has to forward your petition to the Supreme Court and then inform the sessions court of it so that it sits on the warrant of execution. Or else they'll march you off next door and blindfold you before a month is over. And one of the jail clerks has to type out your letter and all the copies that you'd want to send with it. You'd have to massage his calves and oil and crack his toes. And so that he agrees to do it fast...

'Once that SLP's gone and the court is made aware of it, you can sit in that corner and relax and masturbate for the next four years, give or take another five... Of course, the Supreme Court will not be moved to tears by your whining. It too will confirm the sentence because you're a sweet little lad who butchered six people so as to wolf down their dinners. But when *that* judgment reaches you, if I am around, we shall draft a mercy petition to the President of India. Never say die.'

OCTOBER 8, 1970. CENTRAL JAIL, NARASINH Nagar is turbulent with commotion. The prisoners are scrubbing floors, cleaning toilets, placing potted plants in corridors and sprucing themselves up in readiness for the visit of the new Inspector General of Prisons, Madhusudan Sen.

The IG's redoubtable reputation has preceded him. A stickler for rules and for justice, formidably in the know of things, utterly fearless because certain that the law supports him in all that he does, his is just the sort of personality that annoys and unnerves terribly Shiv Narain Meshram, the jail superintendent. What's his bloody problem? Why can't he leave us alone?

The visit lasts four hours. With the meticulousness of a diligent clerk, the IG himself pores over registers, points out discrepancies in the accounts, personally inspects the toilets and the kitchens, tastes the lunch, compares the conditions in the wards with the provisions of the Prison Act and the Jail Manual, verifies the medicines in the dispensary against the stock ledger, speaks separately to several groups of prisoners, jailers and wardens and makes the Superintendent very uneasy with his questions.

'I see that you have kept four prisoners in solitary confinement for periods ranging from eighteen months to six years. The Act gives you powers in this matter for a specific duration of? Would you by any chance know?'

'A … a … a fortnight, sir … I—I will review the position at once, sir.'

'Let me speak to one of them. This Basant

Kumar Bal fellow, for example. Why is he in solitary?'

Meshram can't immediately place the individual. And when he does—'Ah yes, sir, Gomaas!'—he begins to beam at having done so and adds proudly, 'He hasn't had a single visitor in twenty years—' and only then, having remembered that he has been asked a question, returns to it airily—'Oh, some fight or the other, no doubt.' A warden stands on tiptoe to breathe a word in his ear. Meshram nods vigorously, the warden shuffles rapidly out of the room. 'We have just sent, sir—some three weeks ago—a mercy petition from Gomaas to the Honourable President of India. We will show you a copy, sir.'

Madhusudan Sen, waiting in the office of the jail Superintendent to meet Basant Kumar Bal again after twenty-one years, and to read what garbage some other prison inmate has composed and transcribed for him, and made him sign, in his plea to the President, shifts in his chair and looks away at the one single window. Its iron grille has been freshly repainted dove grey but its panes continue to be brown and opaque with grime. Justice delayed is justice denied; true, but justice delayed for twenty-one years is also a gift of two decades of life to a recipient unworthy of even a moment of it. A poor sort of life, no doubt, when it is spent immured behind grey walls and barbed wire, but surely preferable to the cold eternity of death. Sen could see that that would have been the line of argument adopted in the mercy petition. *Honourable and Most Gracious Sir, I genuflect before your Benevolent Knees to submit that I have suffered enough. Please be so munificent as to grant me another two decades in prison.* The fiend. Sen is clear-headed enough not to jumble the sluggishness of the judicial system with the monstrosity of the crime; it demands a commensurate, monstrous punishment. You wait, we'll get you yet.

The slap of slippers in the corridor, slower

now; perhaps the warden is not used to rushing after anything. He pauses in the doorway to stiffly half-bow to Sen before stepping up to Meshram to hand him a file covered in brown paper. Meshram pretends to read its first two pages without actually seeing anything and then reverentially places it, open, before the Honourable IG.

Sen bends forward to examine its contents. 'It seems to be addressed to King George VI.'

From the other side of the desk, Meshram cranes his neck to an impossible length to see the yellowish page in front of Sen's extended forefinger; he then nods to confirm to himself that indeed the IG has not been lying. 'That's the template, sir, used by several dozen prisoners ever since the forties.' And then, with a reassuring coo in his voice, 'But it will serve its purpose, sir.'

'Which is?' Sen riffles through the pages of hysterical, sycophantic drivel. It might just work. 'Have you informed the sessions court that the prisoner has sent a mercy petition to the President?'

Meshram looks wildly around at his subordinates for the answer. One warden nods his head vigorously. 'Yes sir, we have,' affirms Meshram.

'Personally, I doubt it very much.'

GREY AND LIFELESS, BASANT KUMAR STOOD before the desk and stank. Sen had forgotten the face and wouldn't have recognized him but he realized in a moment, with a start that felt like the release of some fluid other than blood in his system, that the restless, bulbous eyes, flitting from desk surface to chair to the photograph, on the wall, of the President, that gaze of the unstable temperament hadn't changed. It was the face of a personality that registered nothing but the fear of physical pain. As far as possible, he would avoid being beaten up; the rest—the idea of the future, of pleasure and human warmth—was a distant, forgotten country.

'I just thought I should ask you,' began Sen, clearing his throat theatrically, 'how things are with you.' He stopped; what he had said sounded so stupid that he was angry with himself. 'You—all of you—will move out of solitary immediately. And I was wondering whether I should, you know, send you—' his offer sounded most odd to him even as he was making it—'some food from outside. As a kind of compensation for the confinement.' He rushed through the rest of it, continuing to feel foolish, but again because he was one to finish what he had started: 'Would you have any preferences? I was thinking of some non-vegetarian item. You would be expected of course to share the stew with the other three who have been in solitary with you.'

Of the two last milestones that remain to be mentioned in this history, the first is dated December 5, 1972.

Warrant of Execution of a
Sentence of Death

To

The Officer-in-Charge of the Jail at Narasinh Nagar

Whereas Shri Basant Kumar Bal, the prisoner in Case No. ___, at the Session held before me, has been, by a warrant of the court dated the 7th day of February, 1956, committed to your custody under sentence of death and whereas the order of the High Court at Nandanpur confirming the said sentence has been received by this court;

This is to authorize and require you to carry the said sentence into execution by causing the said Basant Kumar Bal to be hanged by the neck until he be dead, at 5.00 a.m. on the 4th day of January, 1973, at Central Jail, Narasinh Nagar, and to return this warrant to the court with an endorsement certifying that the sentence has been executed.

Signed/-
Giridhar Dharmadhikari
District and Sessions Judge
Dated: this 5th day of December, 1972.

—

And the last event in this history takes place on the eve of the day fixed for the hanging.

9 pm, January 3, 1973. Madhusudan Sen, now Agriculture Secretary of the State Government, is, despite the lateness of the hour, still in his office on the fifth floor of the Secretariat at Nandanpur. He has finished his work for the day and is mentally composing his New Year card to Arif Dalvi. The rooms and corridors are silent save for the hum of the tubelights, the occasional, distant car horn floating up from the thoroughfares far below and the periodic clicking of the telex machine next door.

His immediate neighbour is the Chief Secretary to the State Government. The great man himself being away at a meeting in New Delhi, his rooms, like the rest of the Secretariat, more or less, have been dark and silent since 5.30 in the evening. Sen too, saying that he needs peace and quiet to work on the minutes of the mammoth Drought Relief Action Plan meeting of the day before, has asked his office staff to wrap up and disappear. Save for one peon (whom it would have been near-impossible to get rid of; how can the Departmental Secretary be present in office and working without any assistance of any kind whatsoever?), he is alone.

Occasionally, the telex next door rouses itself with a clack and a clatter and begins frenziedly to click away. Sen, all ears, waits till it is sleeping again, then summons the peon and asks him to get both of them some tea. The canteen shuts at six in the evening, so the peon has to descend five floors and go out of the building to a nearby dhaba for it. They have had tea twice already since 7.30 that evening. Once the peon leaves, Sen leaves too. He slips out and in to the room next door to see what the telex has to say to the state government. Nothing of interest so far. A reminder from the Department of Expenditure at New Delhi to send the revised Fifth Plan figures for Education and Health. The modified two-day tour programme, beginning January 9, of the Union Minister of Defence Production to Bombay, Bhopal and Nandanpur.

My dear Arif,
Thank you so much for your card. And happy new year to you and your family too. Ever since you migrated to Rawalpindi in 1957, you have never failed to send me two cards a year, one at Diwali and the other at the New Year, no matter where I have been posted, Nandanpur, New Delhi, Calcutta, Geneva. I confess that I have tried to be as regular in responding but have failed miserably!

To answer your question, no, there has been no talk here, as far as I am aware, of the abolition of the death penalty. Whatever put that idea in your head? And in, of all places, Rawalpindi! For my money, in any civilized society, the two should go hand in hand: at symposiums and seminars, there should be impassioned discussion on the need to abolish this barbaric practice and at the same time, on occasion, once or twice a year, some satanic villain should dangle at the end of a rope.

I hope that one will tomorrow. I shall post this card only after I am sure—

Sen is startled by the sudden clacking of the telex machine. The same rigmarole once more: put down the pen, wait for things to quieten down, send the peon away, sidle in next door. But this time, at 9.40 at night, against all odds, it is there, that last move in a death-for-death tussle that has lasted twenty-four years.

Most immediate
Death sentence case
Out Today

Chief Secretary
Government of Narmada Pradesh
Secretariat
Nandanpur

Subject: Mercy petition of condemned prisoner Basant Kumar Bal under Article 72 of the Constitution of India, at present confined in the Central Jail, Narasinh *Nagar, Order of the President of India, regarding*

Sir,

I am directed to refer to the two letters from the petitioner, dated 15.09.70 and 14.12.72 respectively, on the subject noted above and the subsequent reference, vide letter No.7/ Bandi Miscellaneous 10/10-70, from the Home Department, Government of Narmada Pradesh.

The attention of the state government is drawn to the decision of the President of India who, in exercise of the powers under Article 72 of the Constitution, and keeping in view the period of over twenty-three years already spent by the condemned prisoner behind bars, of which two years were passed in solitary confinement, has allowed the mercy petition and accordingly commuted the sentence of death to imprisonment for life. The prisoner may be informed of the orders of the President and further necessary action taken in this regard.

The matter may be treated as most urgent since the letter of the petitioner dated 14.12.72 (referred to above) encloses a warrant of execution of the Narasinh

Nagar sessions court that fixes the day of hanging as 4.01.73.

The receipt of this letter may kindly be acknowledged. Post copy follows.

Yours faithfully,
Debiprasad Sarkar
Joint Secretary (Judicial)

Post copy forwarded for information to: Shri H V Mahipalpure, OSD, President's Secretariat, Rashtrapati Bhavan, New Delhi w r t ID note No. C II—11(2)/1970—CA II dated 26 December, 1972.

But this is utterly appalling, says Sen to himself as he reads the telex through a couple of times. He pauses to weigh matters for a few seconds. Then, very, very carefully, he tears the letter off the machine, all the while murmuring to himself, absentmindedly, a sort of refrain: 'The quality of justice is not strained, the-quality-of-justice-is-not-strained.' He neatly folds and pockets the telex and rearranges, solicitously, the rest of the paper on the machine; when he has finished, it does look as though the order was never received, and that nobody has glanced at any of the other messages for hours.

Back in his room, he drinks his horrible tea and tells the peon to inform the driver that his work is done, that he is at last ready to go. 'And also, that on the way home, if we could just stop by Qayamat's for a minute to pick up some kebabs.'

Acknowledgements

I'd like to thank Professor Arup Surendranath of the National Law School for sharing with me the Death Penalty Report of the School and his invaluable views on it.

I'd also like to thank advocates Amritananda Chakravorty and Mihir Samson for enlightening me on various points of law. If I continue to remain in the dark on certain issues, it's really not their fault.